THE
DREAM OF LEAVING

May 22, 2009

*For Mary -
Delightful meeting
at Groler's!
Sharon*

POEMS BY
SHARON LEITER

MAIN STREET RAG PUBLISHING COMPANY
CHARLOTTE, NORTH CAROLINA

Cover art by Paula Leiter Pergament
Author photo by Sean J. A. Edwards

Acknowledgments:

Grateful acknowledgment is made to the following publications, in which some of these poems appeared:

Atlanta Review: "Cha-Cha to the Finish Line"
Blue Ridge Anthology: "Fame," "Monday Morning"
Cimarron Review: "November"
Defined Providence: "How to Survive a Partial Recovery"
The Georgia Review: "There's Only One Poem"
Letters to the World: Poems from the Wom-po Listserv (Red Hen Press, 2008): "The Dream of Leaving"
Oasis: "High on a Hill," "Monday Morning,"
    "Silence in the Form of a Woman," "Styles of Raking"
Pembroke Magazine: "Just Before, in St. Paul"
P.D.Q. (Poetry Depth Quarterly): "Things That Slipped Away"
Sow's Ear Poetry Review: "How Grandma Got Her Body"
Streetlight: "Crows," "The Cellar," "Cat Time," "In Each City,"
    "Declaration"
Tough Times Companion: "Grieving Place"
The Virginia Quarterly Review: "Fame," "Forgive This Prolixity,"
    "Why Call It Dust?"

Library of Congress Control Number: 2007930981

ISBN 13: 978-1-59948-085-5

Produced in the United States of America

Main Street Rag
PO Box 690100
Charlotte, NC 28227
www.MainStreetRag.com

for Darryl

and in loving memory of my parents,
Albert and Selma Sherman

Contents

I

Still Susceptible

It may be heresy,
but anything even faintly
reeking of younger years
pulls my soul right out of me.

Walk in spring, you're bound
to catch a whiff.
Right away your body
remembers itself:
a body like a lake,
languid, opaque
sapphire, dreaming
in its own desire.

Be mature, you plead,
ripe, like an apple
ready to be picked!
Easy for you to say.
But I've already been.

Releasing the Lamb's Ear

Releasing the lamb's ear from
the shambles of its former self,
the stringy paper stalks,
some curled brown leaves,
a handful of capless acorns,
I am like a woman burrowing
through layers of tissue paper
to the delicate, scented tribute
beneath, fingers seeking
the tastefully understated
card of the sender.

A Ballroom of Time

It seems I am always trying to clear out
a grand ballroom of time, empty of
everything: furnishings, musicians,
even the dancers. All that fills
the ballroom is its own expectation,
but even this has no weight, no fixed shape,
only the carbonated light, bottled
and corked in childhood, fizzing in
through the open windows. Oh, and silence,
silence, of course, gliding beautifully
across the gleaming boards.

The Party I Miss

I untangle limb and brain
from the crushing
goose down of dream,

race to the window
and lift the shade
and let the forest in.

But it's over by then,
they've gone their ways.

Only their whispers remain,

only the swirling of
silken skirts,

the laughter of
time's retreat

and tell-tale dregs of
purple wine

in the chalices of trees.

Things That Slipped Away

our life in Boston
with three kids
and all our oldest friends

sweet sinlessness
never betraying
never betrayed

a thousand colored dream-fish
swimming through the dark
leaving only sparks

but not you,
sweet breather at my side

not you, not yet

In Each City

In every place we've lived
we've had to remake ourselves
from the rubble of disaster.

As if each chosen city
harbored beneath its broad avenues
a huge invisible animal
set to flick its neck
through the concrete
and make a meal of us.

In one city my sanity crumbled,
in another, our marriage,
in a third, our insubstantial
ladder to the stars.

The work it has been
restoring them.

Only childhood saw us gently
to the door, leaving limbs
and dreams intact,
shoving us past
the threshold toward a
green continent
so welcoming,
we saw only later
what was lost.

Scam

Night: the travel adventure
none but the hapless would sign up for:
permanently off-season, rightfully obscure,
easy enough to get to but just try
extracting yourself in one piece.
Slip away unnoticed –
you'll still have to run like hell
from the tenacious natives.

And talk about post-vacation depression!
Days later, you can barely stand up straight
for the weight in your pockets
of those weird souvenirs
you can't name, won't touch and
never bought in the first place.

Just Before, In St. Paul

Ah the streets, the coffee shops, me.
Long curly hair, gold rings, tight jeans.
Wearing my ten thousand blouses
tucked in. The last good trip.
Last town to see the last of me.

Happy as I'd ever been, as I recall,
meaning not very. Puffed by a bit
of money, but still rattling around
in the great Hall of Missing Things.
Hiding the hole. Telling
the tale's top layer. Siphoning off
the cream of the soul
for public consumption. Chasing
the sleep of the blessed
with my netless butterfly net.

And nothing in that northern air--
no faint, steely aroma, no sudden
brutishness beyond bearing
gave warning that this sinking self
would be remembered as the best,
or that the last photographs
would show only a pretty woman
waving from a vanished world.

November

Once more the forest
flings open its doors,
the shimmering banners
of the leaves withdraw,
and the long, intricate corridor,
inlaid with moss and lichen
and lined with innumerable
private chambers,
stretches before me.

All through the darkening days
I stand sentry at the window
and wait for the sudden
presence of the white-tailed deer –
those wary, fine-boned poems of winter –
walking alone or in slow processional.

How Grandma Got Her Body

Not suddenly,
in all its colors
and consistencies.
She would have died of fright,
or, more likely, simply refused
to inhabit such a monstrosity.
She who'd fled tyrants in her life,
outwitted Cossack marauders,
nimbly crossed borders –
think she'd cave in to such an outlaw,
a *paskudnyak*, in a free land!

For years – who knows how many –
longer than she had any right,
she looked down at the smooth
lines of her belly and legs,
and wasn't surprised.
There was an unused girl inside,
a half-forgotten dybbuk,
whose wishes floated outwards
through the woods of blood and bone
to the meadows of the flesh,
and kept them young.

Then one day the sun showed her otherwise:
a wobble in the thighs,
dips and dimples
no one should know from.
From then on, as the saying goes,
it was all downhill,
but so slow,
at such a gentle angle,
who could notice?

She had eyes, of course, she saw:
too much of her and all wrong:
lumpy as an old mattress,
spotted as a hen,
her secret *tsorros*
risen to the skin,
in swollen blue rivers.

But bring herself in for repairs?
Don't even mention it!
She should have herself
trimmed, cauterized, bleached
like a stained tablecloth?
For what?
So the clock should tick backwards
a crooked minute?

Instead, she welcomed the body
like the companion of her widowhood,
fed it and slept with it,
shtupped it with pills, listened
to its tales and told them
to all comers,
until at last
she sat within it,
if not exactly comfortably,
then with a kind of
ferocious satisfaction.
The body gloated from her black, Russian eyes.

To the end, they called her beautiful.

Cha-Cha to the Finish Line

I'm panting through the final
rounds of that marathon
my parents danced

into their nineties,
heads erect, hips obedient,
so what if the music was indistinct,
the others dancers a blur.

Of course, they lived in easier times.
All they had was two World Wars,
a Great Depression,
and Existentialism –
which they never heard of.
They had Frank Sinatra
in boyhood mode.
They had the Ed Sullivan Show.
Oh, let's not go there.

They had it tough.
Polio. No antibiotics
until their thirties.
Who knows why they
lived so long, so zestfully,
while I,

with all the benefits
of higher education
have been stumbling
around in the bad dream
of a dread disease
I'm sure I caught
from my innocuous upbringing.

How come they cha-cha-d
to the finish line, the same steady
characters we always knew,
while I've been stopping
and re-starting myself with
ever waning expectations
for the past decade?

Maybe they were inoculated
by all the hard times
against what was to come.
Maybe they'd called each other
"kiddo" so often in the thirties,
that's who they stayed –
wise guys, good sports,
Dapper Dans and hard-edged
heroines with hearts of gold.

Dying and limping and losing
were not in the scenario, so they put off
thinking about them until the last
failed surgeries and ended, hoping.

When Daddy chose me for the dance
I stepped right out
though I could never
do that little hop he and Mama
slipped into the rhythm,
that thrilling half-step, theirs alone,
gesture to a private music.

Cancellations

That year the grand regatta
of the seasons was cancelled
for lack of attendance. The days broke
into small choppy waves
where no boat ventured.

The eyes of the calendar
went milky blind,
the better not to see
what would not happen
and every time I tried
to jot some rendezvous
or celebration
my ink went dry.

Where can I plan for you now?
Where intercept you?
All that seems to be left is
storage and distribution.
Who shall have this or that piece of you?
What images shall I adore?

No matter the attic of my house
is crammed with incarnations.
I need a sign of you in a definite weather:
a bit of unexplained smoke drifting
through the breathless air between branches.

Declaration

The dead tree stood
impervious in the wind that
danced the living.

While reams of leaves locked
easily into the fury's fingers,
sap in branch and trunk
inclining raptly toward
that green rhapsody,

the dead tree stood
spectral in its place,

then spoke
itself
in a swift
soundless keel,
a snapping at the base.

The Cellar

I went down the wooden stairway,
trying to remember the one loose step,
and wandered blind in the windowless cave,
my desperate fingers seeking
the string beneath the naked bulb.
An iron table stacked with Grandpa's
faintly sinister, unliftable tools,
the waiting nooses of unused clothes lines,
a graveyard of abandoned sleds and bikes,
and in the rear, more hair-raising
than horror comics, more gothic
than my imagination,
lurked Grandpa's coal bins
where black, glittery mountains
rose in pinnacles, and Grandma's
locked, forbidden storage
bins where years later,
the flower of my college library
would molder and turn to ooze,
not even Proust or The Complete
Shakespeare surviving
the rising waters
that drowned
the last,
blackening treasures
of that immigrant lair.

Thinking of Leaving

How could I leave you, even in sleep,
pitying you as I do?

Didn't you arrive with me,
covered in feces?

Weren't you buried alive in
chicken pox weeks later?

Haven't you borne the brunt
of all my excesses,

bent like a stunted tree
beneath my griefs?

Haven't you played
like a demented orchestra
beneath my baton?

You had rhythm –
I'll give you that.
You had ecstasy.

Someone else could have
loved you better.

You were never quite up
to my standards.
Never sexy, athletic,
amoral enough.

And now, when you lock the doors
and windows, loosing
the poisonous fumes through
all our rooms,
what am I to do?

Head for some hidden refuge,
rush up the ladder with no rungs?

Or breathe, as I have
always breathed – with you?

II

Monday Morning

Step aside, clear the aisles,
while my wits reassemble
from every far point
of the globe. Must I say
what you know? The hostess
of dreaming would not let me go.

Though we ate your fine dog
several nights in a row,
we had quite enough left
for a pet, and he slept
on the porch, blending
in with the walls.

I bought and I bought,
though the check that I signed
wasn't mine. It was my turn to hire
and I told you the winner was you,
should the money come through.

Once I swear I could hear
the first ting of a ring
from the world at the top
of the stairs. But the straw of
that ladder of sound shredded thin,
left me no way back in.

Now I pray for the power
to open one eye, late for a life
I know nothing about.
Drugged by the heat
of a beating heart,
on the pure white beach of time.

The Beast

There is a beast
at the bottom of the water
and it breathes.

The shape of the beast
is unimaginable.
I mean this literally.
You cannot twist your mind,
your will, your litany of language
around the shape
of this beast.
The thought of naming it?
A joke.

Still, do not despair.
The beast breathes.
From the flood of bubbles
it sends up, some few survive
and cling to the fine line
dividing wet from dry.

If you've the slightest
skill in prophecy
from all your years in
the world, garner some tale
from those tiny eruptions.

It won't be true.
It won't be the one that was told.

Still, do it.

If nothing else, you'll understand
the roiling of the water
came, not from the weather
we walk in, but from the deep,
buried shape of belief.

Silence in the Form of a Woman

Silence in the form of a woman
fills my bed
and while her limbs
lie white and mute,
a chattering jungle of memories
fills her head.

Though she is ill and going
nowhere she has known,
untiring, she gropes from
vine to hairy vine,
alighting just beyond that din,
where green grows sparse
and tenuous as time,
and something else begins.

House of Remission

This time I'll be a cautious guest:
No flinging my legs onto the velvet sofa,
no making believe I've always lived here.
This time I'll watch my step.

And I'll watch what I touch.
There's that thumbprint of destiny
tattooed on my skin. What if
it rubs off on the furniture?
Who would invite me then?

Above all, no after-dinner rant
about *the whole long nightmare,*
must have been some kind of accident.
No one, not the reticent host,
the other uneasy guests,
nor the gods in the woodwork,
believes in accidents here.

Prayer of Middle-Age

God of my best childhood memories,
help me now.
Who else can I turn to
in the sweet empty paradise
of my heart?
                    Who else
console me for fortune better than most?

Ignore the fact I never knew you,
that what I worshiped was the light.
God of my godless childhood,
help me now.

For, where I stand, the days
before me may be few or many,
with no one to foretell it.
And where I live, the value
of my flesh declines
with each new accident of time.

god help me, God of Life,
I know the years you gave
were more than dreams,
but something dense that
intervened between the cramped,
early rooms and these, so grand
I wander through them on a journey.

But as they passed, those years,
they turned their backs,
they closed me out
until their memory and heaven merged.

Dear Lord of Loss, there's room enough
within your gift for all I've loved,
but few who come. The old move carefully
within their skins, they balance in their ruts.
The young give us their plans, their pain,
but so few days.

I know, God of Disaster, self-pity has no place
in destinies so mild as mine.
If I could only learn to waken
without grief. If I could just let go,
fling wide the doors,
prepare a table for whoever wanders in.
If I could learn to gather
what remains of laughter
from a stranger's lips.

High on a Hill

High on a hill in the middle of France –
a distant mansion.

To reach it I would have to
swim an English Channel
of grief, and I am
no athlete.

I'd have to part with
everyone older or frailer,
with a wardrobe of old selves,
and I am known
for hoarding.

I'd have to lose –
and losing makes me wild –
all of the rooms of
the long dream
I shared with you.

I'd waken in my large bed
and the lifelong
weakness in my chest
would wrap me
like a thick robe.
I would belong to it.

I wonder if the cats –
those new, unnamed ones –
would comfort me.
If sunlight would,

or the sound of the trees.

White March

The woods are mild, yes,
but with the odorless mildness
of the house,
without a single
soul-churning aroma.

The gray bones of the oaks
stand motionless
against the flat white sky.

The crows rage past my window
like hysterical theater directors,
berating the players,
the sound crew,
the scenery painters.

Distant tittering.

The crows know something.

The white curtain of the sky
refuses to rise.

The Deer Are Not Enough

When we first came to the woods,
the deer were emissaries
from a hidden kingdom.

But now the deer are not enough.

They were masters of unheralded
appearance, whole in an instant.

But now we watch their slow approach.

When our eyes locked, they would
vanish utterly, who knew when to return.

Today they hover at a coy distance.

Watching them gather beneath my window
 one snowy twilight,
I stood within a blazing hall of wonder.

Now I watch them fondly as they graze.

I long for peacocks, small black bears.
And yet, should Pliny's unicorn
with feet of elephant and tail of boar
spring thunderous from the forest,

I'd soon be listening for his footfalls,
lumbering up the leafy hill,
and sniffing at the air to catch
the stench he trails
up to my porch, from other worlds.

Getting Through Spring

The woods will manage splendidly.
Never prioritizing,
never juggling deadlines,
wholly unruffled at falling
behind or, more likely,
getting a little
ahead of themselves
as mild March winds
spur the eager blossoms to the
brink of flowering.

Standing always
where they were meant
and knowing when
they will come
to the end of themselves.

More than the sum
of their tiny
flittering
terrors.

Never divided
between flowering
and dying.

Never dreading
the news of impending
removal from the
heady procession
of their own unfolding.

My Mother the Naturalist

Animals have such sad faces,
says Mother for whom
animals in general
are edible or not,
somehow *trayf*,
beyond the pale,
or swiftly spiteful
like the cat she put on her head
in the darkness of Russia
that made her hair fall out.

What should they do? I ask her,
pointing at the white-tailed deer
who have materialized
in the woods behind our house,
grin when they see the corn?
Their faces don't work that way.

Don't be so smart,
and don't get too close,
she says, freezing in place,
then fleeing with
animal grace
into the darkness
of the house.

III

Daddy Sold the Car

Gave it away, more likely,
to his no account son-in-law.

Walked right away from his driving days.

Counted his profits in lesser losses.
No gas, insurance, taxes,
no more cocking his bad ear
to the sound of trouble coming.

Sure Mother agreed.
You should hear how relieved.

Solly can drive us to the doctors.
And what? You never heard of car services?
Two bucks to Waldbaum's and back.
What could beat that?

Sure I remember buying the--whaddid
you call it?--the everglade green Mercury,
and the way you girls screamed
when I pulled the wad of hundreds
from my pocket. Who had credit then?
Who even heard of it?
Sure I remember all those trips
to Manhattan, the beach, the mountains,
whatever you girls wanted.

Sharon, Sharon,
a time comes and goes.

And where do we go these days anyway?

Rockaway in the Himalayas

I imagine the eighties
as a high Asian
mountain range,
steep icy peaks
tracing an erratic cardiogram
against the thin sky.

"How the hell we got here
is beyond me,"
Daddy might say.
Yet here they are,
breathing
the rarified air,
panting and
paling and
fainting from
time to time.

Mostly, though,
Mother putters about
on the snowy slopes,
Daddy lounges on
the Barca of a
slick ledge.

The cold, they figure,
is in their bones.

If either of them knows
how exposed they are,
no roof,
no walls,
no place to go,
stars so close
they nibble your earlobes,

they don't say so
in front of the children.

Rockaway in the Virginias

They waken in their new rooms,
freshly aired, repainted,
cleared of the last, demented
tenant's junk, the pale beige rug
purged of coffee, urine, blood.

They wash. Slowly undo the
fatal to confuse medicine
tubes, spitefully labeled
in gibberish syllables.

Just like at home,
Mama scrambles Daddy's
eggs in butter substitute,
pours him hot, weak instant.
They eat in half-light,
blinds closed against
that vanished Northern ocean
that enthralled their middle years.

Here, the humid nights are empty
of sirens and backfires.
Nothing but crickets.
Carrying on like nobody's business.

Nothing to do but sit on cushioned benches
beneath a canopy dripping
with pansies, twisting their necks
to grasp the edgeless murmurs
blown from the lips of their
dandelion-headed companions

We heard better in New York,
where people talked better, says Dad.

While Mama tells him,
less in sorrow than in wonder,
how all the *goyishe* Southern ladies
are the same: so tall and thin
and with the same long face.

Oh, yeah? he laughs.
 Since faces, lately, are a blur,
he'll take her word for it.

A whole new life, he'd told
his daughter, on the drive down.
And though he's yet to see a *real* sidewalk,
much less one paved with gold,
like the greenhorn he'll always be,
he can't help hoping.

An Afterlife in the Catskills

I like to imagine you
living just one day
again and again
beneath a still warm sky
like this one, a day
of your soul's choosing
unmoored from past or future
so that whatever you're doing
you could go on forever.

I like to think you're poling
your raft down the hidden
river that lay at the leafy
center of your life.

But maybe you're only walking
down a road like this one,
breathing green grass smells,
New York voices chattering
in the trees. Your coltish legs extend
from big-checked shorts,
your brown unspeckled chest glitters
with fresh sweat, the long fingers
of your right hand, still swathed
in a black handball glove,
swing idly at your sides.

Ah, no, you're closer now, I see
you're in your work clothes,
looking a bit green from the road.
You're holding something—a box from
Ebinger's, a hot watermelon from the City,
one of your infinite gifts.
You've put the packages down.
You're stooping now, lifting a child,
high, into your heaven.

To the Old Ones,
Outdoors, Airing

Wisps of bone, loosely linked
beneath a fragile coverlet of skin,
your faces lift and drift upon
the passing breeze
of faceless greetings. Each nod
dispels the wizard's smoke,
renders you visible
within the rushing density
of younger lives.

And so you smile, content
to know yourself revived
within the oval moment
of hello-goodbye, and ride
serene upon each footfall's
fading wake, and hear once more
your first, enduring name.

The Boxer

for my father

Like a k.o.'d boxer forever rising
by the count of ten, shakier each time,
fetching fewer beauties from the world,
your body lets you lead it to its corner.
You wipe it down and give it water,
doing all you can before the next assault.

Your sorrow isn't for yourself,
but for this washed-up warrior
who won't retire with dignity
but drags you from city to city,
fighting for his old crown.

Whether from love or loyalty
or just plain habit, you go along,
you've managed him too long
to leave him now.

I watch you, ringside, eyes dulled
with the same desire as his,
crazily elated by a good punch.

Sent Away
for my mother

You who gave me rooms
now have only the half of one
wedged beside a wide, papered corridor
where people wander, seeking their places
on a plain without landmarks.

Like dogged travelers,
they seek a path through
the unlifting fog,
asking directions only
by taking the wrong one.

Somewhere not far
where bibs as big as blouses
wait beside the silverware,
a sweet-faced former diva
sirens the dinner hour.

The old ladies at your table
nod off before the main course,
their heads lolling like heavy flowers
on ragged stems.

Frankly, you say, *I expected
a better quality of health
among the women here.*

My second greatest fear is
that you'll never get used to this,
that for the next ten years
you'll greet me with the hopeful face
of a child at summer camp,
waiting to be retrieved.

My greatest fear is that you will.

Sinking

I watch you as the quicksand slowly gains.
You seem to know how struggle sinks you faster.
The shadows part only to close again.

Once hope's abandoned, what remains?
I can't consign you to your room of shadows,
stand frozen as the quicksand slowly gains.

How can I watch and not feel shame –
you were the one who let me know I mattered –
as shadows part only to close again?

The daughter I would be, would take your pain,
not dull you with this nervous chatter,
not clock you coldly as the quicksand gains.

What were those sun-drenched, early days
when you were light to me and laughter,
if shadows part only to close again?

If light and love were one, you'd see my face.
What radiance remains is all that matters.
— Oh, can you feel me close as quicksand gains,
as shadows part only to close again?

All There

A stranger sat with you
that last day of your life,
a girl with light-hearted pink hair –
just a thing she did on a dare,
something *you* might have done,
given the right century and
decade to be twenty.

She was the last of the parade
of young women who looked,
in a series of exciting coincidences,
just like Julie, the wayward
grandchild you loved like no other.

You were a wild one yourself,
or would have been, if not
for your shtetl conscience.
All your tales were of madcap
adventures gone tame, with
you in the role of sexpot shlimazel.

Your pink-haired friend couldn't get enough.
She lapped you up, this midwestern waif
who'd never known an old person.
You were a revelation.

To Lisa, you whispered,
I have the most gorgeous doctors.
She told me later, radiant. That's how I know
you were all there, that last day of your life.

And you were right, Mama, I noticed, too.
Every last one of them gorgeous,
young, half in love with you.

The Face

The mouth was agape,
skin like graygreen gills,
eyes stunned and unseeing.

They said you were
as good as dead. Machines
were doing whatever it took
to get you a low pass
on life's qualifying exam.
Once unhooked you'd flunk
in a matter of hours, they said,
and not to be surprised
you'd go on breathing a bit
after the monitor screen went blank.

That night I held your hand
through the long, relentless downgrading,
asking forgiveness, not for finishing you,
but for lifting my eyes to that face.

Grieving Place
for Alice

I call and ask *how are you*
meaning *where* and is the air
breathable? I ask
for your coordinates
and can I come there?
Can you call out to me
and *will* you? seeing that
speech is less now
than the sounds of
a house settling
around an emptied room.

You say you're no place in
particular only digging
through an hour and then
another in the fragile
tunnel of time. You're
moving slowly. One slip
of the shovel could
bring down the mountain.

Subway to Manhattan

Never let go of my hand,
you warned me and the sister
I lost in the years beyond that *never,*
as we stood sweating
in our good outfits
of velvet and tweed,
swaying in white anklets
and glossy maryjanes
while the howl rolled slowly
out of darkness.

I can still feel your
white-gloved hand in mine,
the fine blond hairs
on my thighs going taut
as the steel-driven air
lifted our skirts around us.
Then dazing silence,
the sliding of doors
and your grip,
purposeful now,
leading us into
the dingy compartment
where you'd search out
three scratchy yellow
straw seats together
or two plus your lap,
mine to claim as the younger.

Where we were headed I
scarcely recall, except that
the city streets were gray
and stone and formal.
You had to dress for them,
as for your welcoming
into the world of consequence.

Yizkor

for my parents

I've got a non-stop service mumbling in my brain,
more hungry, more implacable than Yom Kippur.
As long as voices murmur, I remain.

I can't relinquish what I can't contain,
and so I daily practice to endure
the ancient service chanting in my brain,

lament entwined with sacramental praise
of time's enchanting, chilling roar.
While yet the voices murmur, I retain

that part of me that's buried in your grave,
and know again the whole we made before
the train of mourning rumbled through my brain,

slicing the landscape into now and then.
You go on living at the core.
As long as voices murmur, I remain

a link within the severed golden chain
that praise or pain will not restore.
A nonstop service mumbles in my brain.
Within your vanished voices I remain.

Welcome to the Calendar
of Memory

Once more we've things
to plan for, Dad:
small ceremonies,
half in English,
half in that prayer book Hebrew
that always made you
feel like an ignoramus,
now the language
of your absence.

Not much to eat or drink
at these gatherings
but the salt taste of your ocean
still lingering in the air.
The program's simple.
You wave to me from a distance.
I weep, reciting the words
I need to lead me deeper
to that altar where
a single burning verb
links us in tense eternal.

IV

The Roots of Emptiness

The roots of emptiness,
if settled shallowly
in sandy soil,
may lift away
on the same taxiing winds
that dropped them off.

And if they've burrowed
somewhat deeper,
strong fingers or a simple tool
should toss them clear,
their crab-like tentacles
flailing the air.

Then there are those you never see,
roots buried coffin-deep and tied
to the core of the globe
by iron strands.
Their black flowers flourish
everywhere.
Spot one in time and, like a tic,
you can pry it loose, careful
not to leave the hair of a root
embedded in the skin.

Barring such vigilance,
you are lost, once again,
for the length of their black season.

April Sickroom

Nothing makes me
more of a child
than waking alone
in the cracked smelly bowl
of a bed in the
great lukewarm
soup of illness.

Swim, swim! say the old reliable
voices of the sickroom.
Fling your feverish
limbs toward the rim.
Clear the snot-filled tubing!
Get set for body renewal!

Mommy and Dad have gone
off to work in the fields
of graveyard.

Neighborhood's dead.

Even the gray-sided cube next door
noisily turning itself into a house has
grown silent, the little helmeted
figures, dangling from windows
and banging dwarflike within –
nowhere in sight.

But, see, the blue castles of the ajuga
begin to sprout on the slope of the hill
and, though their brown veins give me pause.
I'm expecting the trees at any moment.

Why Call It Dust?

The body is the true divinity,
leaden and winged at once,
fearful and merciful,
terrible in its veiled,
relentless intentions.

The body knows
how to be born,
how to grow,
how to transpose
from borne to bearer,
how to suckle, how to sicken,
how to explode with pleasures
the timid soul won't sanction,
how to hold on until
the final minute,
how to let go.

These legs and feet go
swinging by beneath me,
lively, imperative,
bearing me where
I must go, while I,
I might be whistling
down a distant road.
Day or night,
with or without
its sleeping passenger,
the body travels on.

The Dream of Leaving

It was a life.
The waking and sleeping,
the slow train journeying
over the mountain, steaming
again and again into still,
pleasant stations
whose name-plates told us
we lived what
we'd never planned.

And endless brave
mornings when we'd go
again, only to learn
how space is curved
to the contours
of the Mobius fate
that returned us
at nightfall
to the old house,
the dream of leaving,
the hours that sucked us,
moth-like, into each other's
arms and eyes and mouths.

I cannot wrap
these fourteen years
going on fifteen
going on infinity
into a gala package
for God's eyes,
saying, *this we did,*
it wasn't enough, this is gone.

I cannot become
that camera
that snaps us in
terrible poses
for future museums
to sort and discard.

I'd rather stay
sunk with you here
in the great animal fate,
the tall grass around us,
the summer smells,
the orchestra of insects,

longing for where we are,
going wherever we go next.

Crows

This is a room,
nest with a roof,
several layers
of insulation
separating
self from sky.
This is the slippery
stretch of time
known as alone.
Might've been silent
without the crows
yammering. *Black anger*,
they cry, weighting
the bony branches
with something warm
and definite. Common coin
of the wintry world, they fall
toward my eyes like blindness.
They're what I've got, without trying.
Crows, I say, when they stand
upon my path. And nothing
lifts in me, and nothing grows,
until a tiny,
feathered music box
flits into view,
peers about, as if pursued,
utters its paradise tune,
once, twice, thrice,
and vanishes.

Goals

You are walking
out your time
in this world,
among the walls,
the photographs,
the furnishings.
Not that you're
merely decorative
or functional and
timed like the kitchen
appliances. No.
You are the mistress,
the witness.

This tall cedar
house is your
Greatest Show
on Earth,
humming
beneath the tent
of winter stars.
You're running
a small kingdom,
of memories,
of mercies.

Yes, yes, you have
paper errands you call
your work. You make
a journey of them,
but all the while
you're at home,
the house your
true membrane.

Me

Times, when the fear,
casting off dream's befuddling masks,
its trunkfuls of buskins and padded sleeves,
stabs through my sleep,

the thing that is me
gapes at the naked blade
and begs for reprieve.

Other times, when I am all eyes,
when neither my skin
nor my history enters in,
when I am voice
and visions gleaned
from greater memory,
and someone's comfort,

then, even my name
and the name of my death
seem little to do with me.

A Poem about Money

will always be a poem about something else,
about blunder and regret, bartering time and buying off death,

about our long, insoluble, insolvent marriage,
declaring for passion, scornful of money, but savoring

its journeys, its perfumed delicacies, the pleasures
of plundering its paper kingdom in the name of freedom.

A poem about money will measure the distance we've run

from childhood's starting line, ask how did our parents,
for all their lowbrow limitations, do so much better?

At its hungry center, a poem about money will be a poem
about heaven, about how, if we had it in abundance,

God would reinvent us, give us flat bellies and clear complexions,
rock us to sleep in a white house, beneath stable stars.

A lovely green suit of money would enshroud us, ensure us
the right to vanish slowly, at our leisure in familiar rooms.

We might even buy ourselves a final round of kindness,
two short-term tickets to visibility in somebody's eyes.

Cat Time

for Seymour

Come on.
Come to my bed.
No, I will not desert you.
This is my time to observe you,
that I may mourn you properly
when you are dead.

Each morning
you pick a different
part of me
to warm,
laying your great,
furry weight
on chest, belly, legs,

on best days staring
into my face, purring
as if all life's pleasures
could be sucked
from my touch.

And you have rejoiced me
by resuming your old habit
of kneading the covers,
just as if you still had
the claws I had taken from you,
to make you more mine than Nature's.

I will remember you
in all your glory,
best of all three creatures
I have buried,

perhaps because I stopped
to hold you. This time
I could not hurry.

But what if I go first?

It is that time.
Your short span
may yet exceed mine.

Then wandering
the high-ceilinged rooms
of this house,

will you be cold, dense,
immured to any moment
but the present,

or will a small,
mute corridor of memory
go whispering within you?

What Will Remain

for my grandson Jacob

I love the idea of dying
within you, so quietly
you'll never know
who was there.
You'll remember a door
opening and morning air
fresh as the wonder born
over and over again
as I say your name.

And a notion in you
begins to form,
wordless at first,
that the earth holds you
precious, that the sky
and trees and all the names
we learn were made for you
and you for them.

Of all the colors we learn,
I'd like a single one to
settle deeply, weave through
the fertile carpet of the seasons
darkening in the forest.

I'd like to be there in the ember
that stirs within you,
telling you how the earth sleeps
and how it endures.

Not that the light will be
my invention,
or even my memory,
but that between us,
we set it burning.

Retreating

I don't want this hotel
to be in a foreign country.
I don't want to be sitting
alone over my coffee,
chin sleek, raised,
pointed like the prow
of a ship toward
open waters.

I don't want to turn,
half-bitter, half-relieved,
away from love and
its cobweb cells,
its corridors of self-
forgetfulness.

What I want is to retreat,
like the queens
of old, when fertility
has passed and the pleasures
of power gone stale.

A simple cave, maybe,
with running water
and room service.

A secular convent
with mountain views.

Surely you could spare me
for a season or two.
I would return in good time.
I would grow weary of myself.
I would once more be
your handmaiden.

Akhmatova Hungered

Akhmatova hungered
for hungerless
old age
when the tyrant's
monument –
a quivering
half-visible
phallus –
would at last
be toppled
from its
granite base,

leaving her free
to wander
the streets of
St. Petersburg,
emptied of mists,
without the boot-toe
of desire
at her back.

Flesh enveloped her
aging body,
but did hunger
retreat? Did her
undeceived eyes
see a gray ailing city,
her untrammeled
feet stumble
in the dance?
What rhythm
moved her
when those blithe
unstoppable ponies
forgot to prance?

Stone in Shoe

Days when I'd limp about
with a tiny stone
lodged between leather and flesh,
and the pain, slight at first,
would pass warmly
through my ankle bone
and rise, a small flame,
through the ganglion trees
of calf, knee, thigh,
ignite in my groin,
rage in my breast.

And not until somebody said,
It's the stone,
could I stoop to remove it.
The minute I fingered
the hard, flat fragment,
shard of an ancient vessel,
the fire died. The forest inside,
unseared, glowed with a rare light.

Forgive This Prolixity

We haven't spoken in so long.
I had forgotten how to talk
and now I practice in my sleep.
I surge with speech.

For all those years, you see,
it wasn't a matter of words.
Of words I had plenty
and scattered like confetti.
Words sprang from the
anxious sweat of my skin,
buzzed in the heated circuits
of my brain. Words buried
me in strange terrain.

And I forgot whatever it was,
once, in an empty room,
I was desperate to tell you,
before the slow, insidious
journey away.

Fame

for Darryl

Let the big waters wash over us.
No one will know we were here
in the small offices of our souls,
gathering the light that floats
on motes of dust.

Others were quoted,
placed in the stone pantheon.

Yet we, too, ran our fingers
through glittering strands
of star hair,
tippled on mysteries,
murmured beloved theories.

Oh, yes, we were there with them,
sporting in the same
celestial playroom.
And if the world took little notice,
how should we complain?
Busy as we were
in the only universe we knew,
through the briefest of eternities,
celebrating our fame.

If I Sing

Perhaps if I sing
through the last
fat season,
the song will echo
through the thin.

An echo myself and
thinning to ether,
won't I wind myself
in that moth-eaten mantle,
letting it warm me like mink?

What more will I need with
a body long in retreat
to the far peripheries
of vigor, a rodent mind
nibbling the smelly
rinds of reason?

I can almost see
myself humming within
the song, a sailor's tune,
drunk on the sun
and wind, floating
the last flimsy lifeboat
out to sea.

How to Survive
a Partial Recovery

Think of what has returned,
not what has gone forever.

Assume a benevolent shortsightedness.
See only as far as you are there.

Pretend you belong to a race
of handless women. Their eyes
are enough, their lips, their hair.

Remember the young girl
whose angry eyes lashed you
as she rolled in her permanent chair,
while your own unleashed legs
took you anywhere.

Let Nothing Happen

If events are joltings,
disruptions, sunderings,
then I wish for
a broad wheat-swayed
plain of eventlessness,
each season stretching
faultlessly into the next,
like blank-eyed children joining
hands in a circle of peace.

Then I wish for a morning
such as has always been,
varying only in degree
of dream fatigue,
of coffee bitterness,
of willingness to lift
rabbity eyes to
the latest fairy-tale of
somebody's sleepy head
vanishing from his shoulders
in a mythical kingdom
beyond the seas.

Proposal to the Dead
for my parents

After all these months of trying
to live without you, I'm still
unwilling. So what if you
moved in with me?
Let my home be your home.
Since I can't exclude you, come
with me through my days.
Say what you always said and
stand beside me as my eyes
brush the things that need doing.
You were ever the masters of dailyness.
You'd be naturals, even as shadows.
I still hear your steps, smell your
perfumed efforts rising through
these rooms. I can't seat you
at the table again, but be with me,
as I make the meal.

The Harbor

All through the night I cling
to the mast of a dream
that speeds toward a harbor
it never can enter or even glimpse,
though none can doubt that it exists,
who has studied its contours in bold relief
there, right there, on the cartography of wish.

There's Only One Poem

There's only one poem,
and its name,
so far as I know,
is wakening.

It has only one aim,
so far as it has one:
to find the whole house
filling with sunlight,
the floors striping with light,
the windows awhirl with it.

The poem, the house and its light
are silence austere and welcoming,

inviting the poet to step lightly
out from the shadows,
to sift herself, like finest sugar,
sparsely, slowly,
into the delicate
texture of time.

Bright broken morning,

what are you but
an aftermath,
dragging behind you those
thin tinsel bells –
two-thirds of my life on
your raggedy tail?

Seen from some distance
of story, album or archive –
it's finished:
beauty, beginnings,
wholeness and
high adventure,
brilliance,
making a difference.

Still, it's Monday morning,
January twelfth,
at the start of
another century.
White sun on snow in
a soundless neighborhood.
Within the quiet
precincts of a rested body,
the hours yet seem spacious –
redolent cedar chests
set to receive and preserve
the latest bounty
of a listening life.

Special Thanks

Special thanks go to Susan Shafarzek, who perceived the shape of this manuscript, and to Judy Longley, Kenny Marotta and Jean Sampson, who read it at various stages and offered their encouragement and wisdom. Warm gratitude goes to the Rives Street Poets, who, over the years, have nurtured and helped me refine my work.

SHARON LEITER is the author of a volume of poetry, *The Lady and the Bailiff of Time* (Ardis), as well as of two works of literary scholarship, *Akhmatova's Petersburg* (University of Pennsylvania Press) and *Critical Companion to Emily Dickinson: A Literary Reference to Her Life and Work* (Facts on File). Her poetry has appeared in *Atlanta Review, Cimarron Review, The Georgia Review, The Virginia Quarterly Review,* and many other journals. She has published fiction and essays and was the recipient of a 1990 Virginia Award for Fiction. She serves as poetry editor of *Streetlight,* a journal of art and literature for Charlottesville and surrounding areas. Leiter has a Ph.D. in Slavic Languages and Literatures from the University of Michigan and teaches literature at the Bachelor of Interdisciplinary Studies Program at the University of Virginia. She lives in Palmyra, Virginia, with her husband Darryl Leiter, an astrophysicist.